"Maintaining the right perspective and disposition in serving the broken and needy is critical to a Kingdom-focused, Christ-centered approach to poverty work. Dr. Sanders's reflections provide us with a theologically sound and practically wise philosophy of what it means to be a Christ-follower dedicated to seeking the transformation of communities of poverty, wherever we find them. Every person who seeks to do the kind of ministry among the poor that is truly redemptive must read this booklet."

– *Rev. Dr. Don L. Davis*
*Senior Vice President Church Resources, World Impact*
*Executive Director, The Urban Ministry Institute*

*Redemptive Poverty Work*

© 2021. The Urban Ministry Institute. All Rights Reserved.

Copying, redistribution, and/or sale of these materials, or any unauthorized transmission, except as may be expressly permitted by the 1976 Copyright Act or in writing from the publisher is prohibited. Requests for permission should be addressed in writing to:

> The Urban Ministry Institute
> 3701 East 13th Street North
> Suite 100
> Wichita, KS 67208

ISBN: 978-1-62932-513-2

Published by TUMI Press

A division of World Impact, Inc.

The Urban Ministry Institute is a ministry of World Impact, Inc.

All Scripture quotations, unless otherwise noted, are from The Holy Bible, English Standard Version, copyright © 2001 by Crossway Bible. A division of Good News Publishers. Used by permission. All Rights Reserved.

TUMI Press
3701 East 13th Street North, Suite 100
Wichita Kansas 67208

# Table of Contents

About the Author . . . . . . . . . 7

Introduction . . . . . . . . . . . 11

A Brief Theological Reflection . . . . 17

Toxic Poverty Work . . . . . . . . 23

Redemptive Poverty Work . . . . . 31

Rhythms of Life and Poverty Work . . 37

About World Impact . . . . . . . . 51

## ABOUT THE AUTHOR

When people in under-resourced communities experience trauma, the local church can be a beacon of hope. Alvin Sanders learned this from firsthand experience. While serving as an urban leader in the second most violent neighborhood in the country, a tragedy took place. A police shooting with racial overtones rocked the neighborhood.

As a response, Alvin planted an innovative church that continues to care for, serve, and encourage people from all walks of life. Through this experience he discovered his personal mission: to follow hard after God, to love his family, and to invest in those who invest in the poor.

Alvin is a churchman at heart. After church planting and pastoring, he served as a denominational leader with the Evangelical Free Church of America (EFCA) for seven years.

While there he directed the EFCA *All People Initiative*. Under his leadership the EFCA went from 13% of their congregations classified as urban, ethnic, or multi-ethnic to 22%. He also authored the book *Bridging the Diversity Gap*. With his passion for church leaders, his move to World Impact in 2015 was a natural fit.

His educational background includes a BS in Biblical Studies from Cincinnati Christian University and an MA in Religion & Urban Ministry from Trinity Evangelical Divinity School. He earned a Ph.D. in Educational Leadership from Miami University. Since 2004 he has served as an adjunct professor at a variety of seminaries across the nation.

In his free time, Alvin is an avid reader and loves to follow his favorite sports teams. He is grateful for his amazing wife, Caroline, who maintains a counseling practice in their hometown of Cincinnati. They have been blessed with two wonderful daughters.

In November 2017, Alvin was named the President and CEO of World Impact.

# INTRODUCTION

I wrote this handbook to guide you away from toxic poverty work. Throughout my ministry career my passion has been to raise the quality of life for people who live in poverty. When I first began ministry in the 1990s, I met Jimmy (not his real name) and his family through a local church. He had struggled most of his adult life with substance abuse. Eventually, he and his family started to reach stability. Through my connections, I was able to assist him by opening the door for Jimmy to get a job and some transportation. But one day, things went sideways.

I received a call from Jimmy's boss informing me that Jimmy had been absent from work for a week. My colleague and I visited Jimmy's house to find out what was going on. We learned Jimmy had spent the week partying. I was so mad! My colleague had to restrain me from punching Jimmy — it was not my finest hour! Looking back, I do not blame Jimmy for my reaction because the issue was me. Jimmy was just being Jimmy. The problem was that my good intentions were more focused on me, my reputation, and my role in Jimmy's success. My poverty work had turned toxic.

World Impact has a vision to help you use your spiritual gifts to transform communities. We know poverty work is important, and we know you want to serve others. Even though our world treats poverty as an unsolvable problem, you remain committed to the task. You never tire of seeing poor neighborhoods flourish.

At World Impact we have worked with thousands of poverty workers since 1971. **WE DESIRE TO CREATE LEARNING COMMUNITIES OF REDEMPTIVE POVERTY WORKERS.** We do not want you to burn out as you help those in poverty pursue a higher quality of life. We want to steer you away from the common problem of toxic poverty work.

Being a Christian in the service of others requires the proper mindset and work patterns. In addition to defining toxic poverty work and redemptive poverty work, this handbook also suggests practices to establish a rhythm of life that will help you counteract the natural inclination toward toxic poverty work. I've also included a brief theological reflection on empowerment and Christ's attitude toward the poor and wealth.

Doing redemptive poverty work is urgent. Dr. Gina Zurlo, who serves as Co-Director of the Center for the Study of Global Christianity, wrote that "the typical Christian today is a non-white woman living in the global South, with lower-than-average levels of societal safety and proper health care." What is our posture towards her?

For some, the ideas presented will seem organic and simple. Others may be confused as this may be your first exposure to these ideas; but being confused is often the first step to learning something new. If you push through the confusion, you may emerge with new understanding based on the synthesis of your old and new knowledge.

Those of us who are committed to poverty work often fail to think about *why* we do what we do. Use this handbook as an opportunity to examine your values, attitudes, and beliefs about the poverty work you so passionately do. Work through the content with a group of people. Then get started harmonizing your faith and poverty work. This handbook represents both the philosophy we practice at World Impact and the concepts I have learned as a 2021 nonprofit fellow in the Praxis Community (*https://www.praxislabs.org/*). I am thankful for Praxis's investment in me, and I'm eager to share these ideas with you.

# A Brief Theological Reflection

Our ideas concerning those in poverty and their neighborhoods often is a hodge-podge of misapplied Bible verses and whatever media source (Fox, CNN, etc.) we frequent the most. In 2017, The Washington Post and the Kaiser Family Foundation surveyed around 1,600 adults about their attitudes towards the poor. They found Christians are much more likely than non-Christians to view poverty as the result of personal failure. This mentality leads to the poverty-stricken being treated as "projects" instead of people to serve, which is not what God intended.

Whatever situation we choose to engage, the first step should always be to find out what the Bible has to say about it. When it comes to those in poverty, for some reason this step gets left out. This should not be the case. The Bible gives significant instruction concerning how we are to treat those in poverty. I will briefly comment on Old Testament principles of empowerment and then point out two things we know about Jesus: he favored the poor, and he warned against riches.

## *Empowerment*

To empower someone is to provide pathways of opportunity to improve their situation. In the Old Testament we see that:

- Extraordinary attention was to be given towards making sure that justice was done regarding those who were poor (Exodus 23:6; Amos 5:12; Psalms 10:2,9).

- At all times, some fruit and vegetables were to be left in the fields for the poor to gather (Leviticus 19:9-10).

- No interest was to be charged on loans to those in poverty (Exodus 22:25).

- Every three years a tithe was to be made to orphans and widows (Deuteronomy 14:28-29).

- Every seven years farm fields were to rest and not to be used for profit but rather for those less fortunate to gather what grew naturally for themselves (Exodus 23:10-11; Leviticus 25:3-6).

- Slaves were to be freed after six years of service (Exodus 21:2).

- Every 50th year (Year of Jubilee) lands were to revert to their original owners (Leviticus 25:8-17).

## *Jesus Favored the Poor*

We see Christ's special concern for the poor in his earthly ministry. During his time on earth, Jesus did his ministry as an everyday, common person. Biblical historians tell us that his hometown of Nazareth was not looked upon favorably. His birth in a stable was characteristic of people in poverty. Jesus entered and lived in the world in the humblest, most ordinary way imaginable.

As we look forward to Christ's second coming, we must remember his commands to stay ready for his return and to serve the poor as he did. At some point we will have to go before our Lord and make a case for how we treated the poor during our lifetimes. (Matthew 25:31-46). We will have to provide evidence of what we did to create pathways of opportunity for those who live in the condition of poverty. In Matthew 25:35, Jesus equated taking care of people who are hungry, thirsty, a stranger, naked, sick, and in prison as taking care of him. If we take him at his word, this is a serious lesson. If you are not dedicating parts of your life, mission, and money toward those in poverty, start to do so immediately. This is not done to earn salvation, but rather to live considering the grace we have been extended by Christ.

### *Jesus Warned Against Riches*

Our spiritual state and how we view money are intertwined, so it matters greatly what decisions we make concerning our resources. It was a common false belief during Christ's time on earth that being wealthy guaranteed salvation. Jesus emphatically taught against this mentality (Matthew 19:23-30).

According to Matthew 6:24, money is the primary thing we need to guard against becoming an idol. This is easier said than done. Many people tie their socio-economic class to their identity. In fact, there is such a thing of your wealth (or lack thereof) limiting your ability to relate to God. Where that line is, Scripture is not clear, yet we need to be aware that this is a possibility.

The message of Luke 12:13-21 is that money has no owners, just spenders. We should not put our identity in wealth. The amount of money we accumulate does not correlate to the purpose and meaning of our lives. The travesty of the rich man in Luke 12 is that he had no plans for his surplus, other than to gain more. We must not let wealth seduce us.

## Toxic Poverty Work

Rare is the Christian who does poverty work with an intention to exploit people. Many are motivated to see justice for the oppressed. Some are driven by pursuing righteousness. Others passionately desire to see suffering alleviated. We all have good intentions, and having good intentions is a great starting point. But good intentions do not automatically lead to healthy poverty work, because we are vulnerable to our sin nature. **HEALTHY POVERTY WORK BEGINS WHEN WE GRAPPLE WITH THE FOUNDATIONAL WEAKNESS BUILT INTO OUR WORK — THE IDEALISTIC BELIEF THAT WE CAN RESCUE PEOPLE FROM THEIR CIRCUMSTANCES.**

I call it *savior syndrome*, and it is based on placing too much trust in ourselves, despite our fallen nature.

When we fall into savior syndrome, we take on a role God never intended us to have. Through our good works, we attempt to rescue people or neighborhoods in poverty. We should love our neighbors and disrupt the injustices that cause poverty. We should make sacrifices of time, talent, and treasure. But even with these good deeds, we won't receive superhuman powers to rescue people.

We should never be seduced into thinking that advocacy is the center of our existence. Another consequence of savior syndrome is when poverty work becomes our identity. Our identity then is intimately tied to our successes and failures in rescuing. We can also become relationally isolated, only building relationships with those who are involved in our poverty work.

Closely related to savior syndrome is the issue of power dynamics, known as paternalism. The *Oxford Languages* dictionary definition of paternalism is "the policy or practice on the part of people in positions of authority of restricting the freedom and responsibilities of those subordinate to them in the subordinates' supposed best interest." There are two common ways to frame poverty work, and both involve how we see ourselves. Are we a "guide on the side" or a "sage on the stage" when it comes to those we are helping? Our theory of change at World Impact is that the poor are gifted by God to lead their own lives. We utilize the old Home Depot slogan: "You can do it. We can help."

Our society assumes that people who are financially secure are in the best position to advise those who lack financial security. This places the poverty worker in the tempting position to use the power that comes with their resources to manipulate and control those they are trying to help. When we add in factors such as race, gender, and historical injustice, these power dynamics further cause good intentions to morph into a form of oppression.

I once advised a man named John (not his real name) who had a big heart for his neighborhood. His ministry provided food and clothing. At various times people came in under the influence of alcohol and/or drugs. John adopted a policy of not serving anyone who was drunk or high. His intention was good — to encourage sobriety. But John needed to be redirected.

I asked John what type of help or resources he offered to those working towards sobriety. If parents were drunk or high, didn't their families still need food and clothing? John looked as if he had not considered this. I am sure he wanted people off drugs and alcohol, but upon further review, the real issue was that John felt people were taking advantage of him. When someone couldn't kick their habit, it offended *him*; he took it personally. John felt he had worked too hard and sacrificed too much to bless people who did not respect his wishes. John had good intentions, but he had elevated his own interests above those caught in addiction.

There are also the issues of fatigue and even spiritual disillusionment. Doing poverty work is like playing an 18,000-hole round of golf; it's never-ending. An endless list of public charities in the United States are working towards societal transformation, and yet the problem of poverty persists. Over time, Christians doing poverty work may also discover their faith cannot explain the injustices they confront daily. And instead of growing in their faith, they either develop a diluted, lukewarm version or they abandon it altogether. This "deconversion" is often a by-product of becoming weary of doing good work.

An article called *"Goodbye Christ, I've Got Justice Duty"*[1] tells the story of a pastor who realizes how deeply racism affects our world and is intertwined with poverty. The pastor gains a new understanding of how the Christian church has exacerbated racism. And he decides to "cancel" the institution of the church and embrace advocacy from a different perspective. He questions not only his seminary education but the validity of the Bible itself. The story ends with the statement "Justice must be achieved, even if it cost him his faith, which in the end, it did."

In my experience, this story is not an isolated incident. Today, many Christians struggle to understand the value and role of the local church when it comes to poverty work. When I started ministry in 1991, local

---

[1] Emerson, M., 2020. Goodbye Christ. I've Got Justice Duty. [Blog] *The Exchange with Ed Stetzer*, Available at: <*https://www.christianitytoday.com/edstetzer/2020/september/goodbye-christ-ive-got-justice-duty.html*> [Accessed 24 November 2020].

church membership was a given, and the challenge was motivating people towards advocacy. It is the exact opposite now — advocacy is in, and church membership is optional. Frankly, it is alarming how many Christians believe the two do not need to be in sync.

In August of 1973 Dr. Ralph Winter, founder of the U.S. Center for World Mission, gave one of the most influential lectures ever given concerning missions. Entitled *The Two Structures of God's Redemptive Mission*, he defined the two types of organizations (modality and sodality) that God uses in every human society to work towards redemption. Organizations that have proven their worth and stood the test of time, such as churches and denominations, are considered a modality. A sodality is an organization more focused on a narrowly defined mission — a means of expression God uses within a historical moment, such as a Christian mission agency, nonprofit, or parachurch. Dr. Winter's conclusion was that the best pathway towards redemption was for modalities and sodalities to work in harmony. He suggests that God's redemptive activity requires both types of organizations.

**THEREFORE, WE PASSIONATELY URGE POVERTY WORKERS TO PARTICIPATE IN A HEALTHY, LOCAL CHURCH.** Your faith may have you pursuing a vocation as a public-school teacher in a poor neighborhood, an NGO leader in Africa, an entrepreneur who employs formerly incarcerated people, or a volunteer who mentors at-risk kids. Whatever the case may be, your advocacy should be viewed as your formal or informal way of living out the mission of your local church. In the book of Acts, seeking membership in a local church for the purposes of fellowship, teaching, prayer, service, and personal development was a vital part of the Christian experience.

# REDEMPTIVE POVERTY WORK

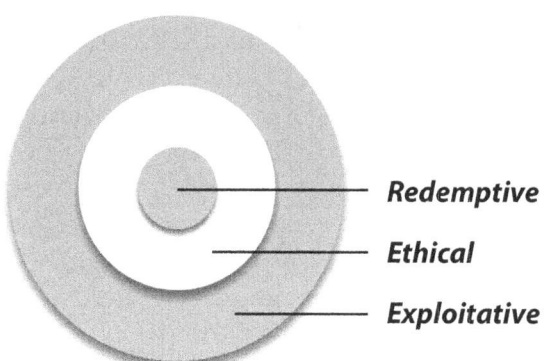

- Redemptive
- Ethical
- Exploitative

Consider the target diagram on page 31 that shows three distinct mindsets when it comes to how we approach poverty work. The *exploitative* mindset on the outer edge produces work that often does more harm than good. People are well-intentioned but fail to properly understand the complexity of poverty and consciously (or subconsciously) put their own motivations above the long-term impact of their work.

Poverty work can give us a sense of moral superiority. It gives us a sense of control over those who live in poverty and the resources available to them. There is nothing we need to do to become exploiters. Unless we intentionally counter this mindset, our poverty work will spring from a desire for control because of our sin nature. Good intentions are not enough.

Developing an *ethical* mindset is a step in the right direction. This mindset is focused on the relationship between the poverty workers and recipients whenever possible. In this mindset, it is no longer about us and our desire to be good and do good. There is nothing wrong with this mindset, and it is often the highest standard for those who are not Christian. Thank God for all those who operate from this space. People who operate ethically have done much good for our society. I call it pursuing the common good.

As shown in the diagram, our goal is poverty work that occurs in the center: redemptive poverty work. **THE REDEMPTIVE MINDSET IS CREATIVE RESTORATION THROUGH SACRIFICE.** Ethical and redemptive work may overlap; both want to serve in a way that brings transformation to people and their communities. However, the difference lies in the motivating force. The redemptive mindset says, "I sacrifice, we win." This mentality encompasses both the recipients of our work and how we employ resources.

It is to love our neighbors as ourselves. It is how we join our story to God's story.

How we choose to sacrifice our time, talent, and treasure is a direct reflection of our spiritual condition. Wealth is a good thing, but if we are not careful, it will seduce us. There is such a thing as having too much or too little, and God wants everyone to have enough to flourish. Therefore, redemptive poverty work is about being as generous as our situation allows. By giving ourselves and our money away, we can redemptively avoid the seductive power of wealth that can lead us away from God's priorities.

The notion of redemptive work is clear throughout the Bible. For example, through his death, Christ paid the price for our lives to release us from the prison of sin. It was not only a past event but is an ever-present, ongoing hope. The theme of redemption found in the Bible has historically been attached to the concept of *Christus Victor*.

*Christus Victor* voices the doctrine that when we believe in Jesus Christ, we are expressing the world-changing idea that Christ came to die for sins, to defeat Satan and destroy his works, and to represent the reign of God in the earth.

How does the redemptive idea specifically apply to poverty work? **POVERTY IS AN OPPRESSIVE CONDITION PEOPLE LIVE IN, NOT AN IDENTITY THEY POSSESS.** Scripture describes poverty as being caused by either personal or societal sin. We have the responsibility to attempt to improve the quality of life of those who live in this condition. Redemptive poverty workers desire more than social progress and more than charity. We work toward the redemption of people and neighborhoods, and we acknowledge God's presence along the journey. We base our advocacy in the understanding that we all need rescuing because we are fallen human beings. We are just as broken, sinful, and weak as those who find themselves in poverty. It is a true understanding of "but for the grace of God go I." Our work reflects a radical solidarity with those who live in the condition of poverty.

Redemptive poverty work puts faith in the supernatural work of God while we attempt the rearrangement of human systemic power. Our faith acknowledges that God is the one who does the rescuing. Our role in the process of redemption is humble advocacy, asking for forgiveness when our own agendas fight for recognition, and admitting our complicity in injustice. Ultimately, the goal of the redemptive poverty worker is to come alongside those who live in the condition of poverty and join in the work God is already doing.

## Rhythms of Life and Poverty Work

Consider what Jesus says our Christian lives are about — loving God and loving people (Matthew 22:37-40). Think of these commandments as the first two parts of the mission of our lives. As poverty workers, we also have a third, unique part. We have chosen to deploy our talents, spiritual gifts, and money to improve the quality of life of those who live in poverty and their communities.

Whether we realize it or not, our faith has been heavily influenced by what is called *The Great Tradition*. In his book *Sacred Roots*, Dr. Don Davis states, "The Great Tradition represents the central core of Christian belief and practice derived from Scripture that runs between the time of Christ and the middle of the fifth century." It is the blueprint of how to center our lives around God. Within The Great Tradition, there are eight practices. They are not just practical; they enhance our poverty work.

**WORLD IMPACT BELIEVES THESE EIGHT PRACTICES ARE TANGIBLE WAYS TO COUNTERACT THE TOXICITY OF SAVIOR SYNDROME, PATERNALISM, BURNOUT, AND CYNICISM FOUND WITHIN POVERTY WORK.** These spiritual practices provide poverty workers with a common foundation while allowing freedom for cultural and personal expression. They are informed by our deepest convictions, and they serve as a basic framework to guide the spiritual practices of our World Impact community.

Undoubtedly, poverty workers will engage in other rhythms and disciplines. View these spiritual practices as an invitation to connect with the World Impact community, an opportunity for self-examination, and a catalyst for spiritual growth. Share them with the important people in your life.

## *A Summary of Spiritual Practices for Poverty Work*

As we acknowledge and confirm the call of the Lord Jesus to invest our lives into those living in poverty, we, the members of the World Impact community, affirm and embrace the following practices, and we commit ourselves to living a Christian life.

### Our Shared Spirituality

We embrace the following dimensions of a shared spirituality:

- **SHARED LIFE.** We affirm and embrace that who we are is more important than what we do. We dedicate ourselves to active participation in a healthy local church, and participation with those we serve by pursuing empowerment, love, unity, and maturity in Christ.

- **SHARED JOURNEY.** We commit ourselves to share a spiritual journey together in a regular rhythm of spiritual practice and observance. This includes fixed times of prayer, taking communion, and observing the church calendar.

- **SHARED DISCIPLINE.** We share an identity centered around practicing the spiritual disciplines of the church consistently and fervently. We will strive for spiritual maturity and Christlikeness as we seek the

Lord in our personal spiritual disciplines of sabbath, personal retreat, tithing, and fasting.

- **SHARED CONFESSION.** We confess our faithfulness to the historic faith, the principles expressed in the Nicene Creed, and testimony that is anchored in the Scriptures regarding the death, burial, and resurrection of Jesus Christ. We hold fast our devotion to the truth of the gospel message as in connection with The Great Tradition of the Church.

## Our Spiritual Practices

Along with our shared spiritual life together, we embrace the following spiritual practices:

**CHURCH MEMBERSHIP.** Today's poverty work occurs during a cultural moment that stresses the universal church over its local expression. Church participation is often seen as optional. We may choose to overvalue advocacy and undervalue the spiritual growth and self-care available in a local church community. Failing to participate in a local church may eventually lead to isolation from the Christian community and a weakening of our faith even to the point of deconversion.

> *Instead of putting our trust in advocacy alone, we commit to active membership within a healthy, local church for the purposes of fellowship, teaching, prayer, service, and personal development.*

*Basic Commitment:* Commit to finding a local church home and attending a weekly worship service.

*Advanced Commitment:* Commit to being an active member of a local church, attending weekly, sharing life with other church members through a small group, and participating in leadership.

**FIXED TIMES OF PRAYER.** Prayer reminds us of God's supernatural power. Our poverty work can deceive us into thinking the injustices surrounding our recipients and their neighborhoods are too much to overcome. We may look at circumstances, ponder what to do, and make God merely an adviser instead of an active participant. We might see our advocacy as the only hope and shrink the role of God within the world.

> *Instead of seeing circumstances as bigger than God, we see God as bigger than the circumstances.*

*Basic Commitment:* Commit to a daily focused time of prayer.

*Advanced Commitment:* Commit to a daily focused time of prayer in the morning and the evening.

**EMPOWERMENT.** Our goal is to empower others, not ourselves. We can limit our resources of time, talent, and money to the boundaries of only what makes us comfortable. We can also pursue situations that will result in benefitting our position more than blessing the recipients of our work.

> *Instead of seeking to increase our personal profile, we work to empower others.*

*Basic Commitment:* Commit to intentionally creating pathways of opportunity for recipients of our work.

*Advanced Commitment:* Commit to a work pattern of 1) understanding the needs of our recipients; 2) helping in a collaborative way; and 3) holding ourselves accountable for results.

**OBSERVING THE CHURCH CALENDAR.** Our poverty work pressures us to view time chronologically. We can be constantly caught in the crisis of the moment. We forget we can sanctify time. We can also forget the many Christians who did the same work as us before we started our journey. We can feel like we are the only ones who passionately care about the poor.

> *Instead of viewing time only chronologically, we sanctify time by connecting our story to the story of God.*

*Basic Commitment:* Commit to following the seasons of the church calendar and reading weekly Scriptures that follow the theme of each season.

*Advanced Commitment:* Commit to following the seasons of the church calendar and reading daily Scriptures that follow the theme of each season.

**SABBATH.** Our poverty work can easily consume us, getting us to become workaholics without any work/life balance. It can rob us of emotional intelligence and relational activities, affecting our mental and physical health.

> *Instead of constant advocacy, we follow a pattern of work and rest.*

*Basic Commitment:* Commit to dedicate one full day every week to completely rest from work.

*Advanced Commitment:* Commit to one full day of rest per week and ten consecutive days each year to completely rest from work.

**Personal Retreat.** Our poverty work tempts us to lose our sense of the sacred. We can forget that we serve to honor God. When we forget this, we lose sight of the fact that holiness is the way to victory. For example, we can also lose our intellectual independence through too much screen time or media consumption.

> *Instead of a life of busyness and distraction, we take time to orient our lives towards obedience to God.*

*Basic Commitment:* We commit to dedicate one workday equivalent (eight hours) every three months for prayer and reflection on our lives and work. During this time, we will disengage from media consumption.

*Advanced Commitment:* We commit to dedicate one workday equivalent (eight hours) every month for prayer and reflection on our lives and work. During this time, we will disengage from media consumption.

**TITHING.** Our poverty work may lead to unrealistic views about money. At worst, we may exploit the stories of the poor to raise more funds. Or we may believe God "owes" us because we make major personal financial sacrifices to reach our goals. We may also lose sight of the fact that a major cause of poverty is economic injustice, which is outside our immediate control.

> *Instead of anxiety about money, or worship of money, we generously give.*

*Basic Commitment:* Commit to giving at least 1% of our total income to our local church and entities that help the economically poor.

*Advanced Commitment:* Commit to giving at least 10% of our total income to our local church and entities that help the economically poor.

**FASTING.** Our poverty work often causes us to search for ways to control situations. Food is one of humanity's basic needs and is often a central point of poverty work. Fasting reminds us that even when it comes to food, we depend on God and God is in control. Fasting can help us see how God meets both our physical and spiritual needs.

> *Instead of seeking control, we fast in response to situations in life.*

*Basic Commitment:* Commit to fast (no food or drink for a 24-hour period) as a discipline against sinful desires once a week.

*Advanced Commitment:* Commit to fast (no food or drink for a 24-hour period) as a discipline against sinful desires twice a week.

I began by stating that I wrote this handbook to guide you away from toxic poverty work. Embrace the reality that our sinful nature leaves us vulnerable to exploitation of those who live in poverty. Renew your mind towards being redemptive as a motivating force for your poverty work. And mature in your faith by implementing the spiritual practices that the people of God have done for centuries. May the Lord bless your efforts!

## About World Impact

### *Who Is World Impact?*

World Impact empowers urban leaders and partners with local churches to reach their cities with the gospel — extending the truth, love, grace, and justice of God in the city.

We believe that the best way to change our world is to declare the hope of the gospel in our cities. The best way to declare that hope is to partner with denominations, networks, and local church leaders. And the best way to partner with them is through relationships.

Our roots go back fifty years to evangelistic kids' clubs — from Los Angeles's Watts neighborhood to Wichita, Kansas, and beyond. As the children we reached grew up, we saw the need for urban churches and the empowerment of church leaders to continue to transform their communities from within.

## *Why World Impact?*

According to the center for the Study of Global Christianity, only 5 percent of the world's church leaders are trained for ministry. Everything at World Impact is focused on training and equipping church leaders — making resources *affordable* and *accessible* to as many as possible. We exist to serve people who minister in communities of poverty — affirming their call and vocation. They are the transforming agents in their community.

## *How Is World Impact Unique?*

*World Impact is perfectly positioned to train urban church leaders.* It champions the ability of the urban poor to own and lead ministry. We believe in the power of community insiders.

*World Impact is kingdom focused.* By focusing on the great Christian traditions rather than on denominational differences, we attract a wide range of like-minded partners.

*World Impact is trusted.* Our decades of experience in urban America bring partners to the table — and donors trust us to get resources in the hands of those who need it.

*World Impact is global because we are local.* Given the increasingly global nature of our country, if we train leaders in major US cities, many will take that training back to their home country, families, and friends.

*World Impact has leverage.* Our staff is impacting even more leaders by being trainers of trainers.

## World Impact's Five Programs

- **CHURCH-BASED SEMINARY.** The Urban Ministry Institute (TUMI) equips and resources urban leaders. It provides affordable and accessible seminary training for men and women in the urban context.

- **URBAN CHURCH PLANTING.** The Evangel School of Urban Church Planting trains, equips, encourages, and enables Christian workers to plant healthy, reproducing churches among the urban poor. This training is designed specifically to equip teams to reach under-resourced communities.

- **TRAUMA HEALING.** Trauma Healing training equips urban ministry workers and leaders to facilitate and host Scripture-based healing groups. Some participants choose to become trained to lead their own healing groups — virally expanding their ministry.

- **PRISON MINISTRY.** Through our Onesimus Workshop, World Impact trains local urban church workers and leaders toward success in discipling those who have been incarcerated. We also offer church-based seminary for those who are behind bars.

- **RETREATS.** World Impact believes in resourcing urban leaders through concise, practical, and hands-on training at women's and men's retreats.

For more information, visit our website at *worldimpact.org*.

Made in the USA
Monee, IL
29 March 2022